O body swayed to music,
O brightening glance,
How can we know the dancer
from the dance?

Yeats, 1923

LENA HERZOG

FLAMENCO
DANCE CLASS

First published in 2004 by Arcperiplus,
98 Church Road, London SW13 0DQ, UK

Publisher: Danièle Juncqua-Naveau
Design: Karl Heiselman assisted by Roanne Adams,
Linda Wade assisted by Sophie Chéry
Managing Editor: Nick Easterbrook
Assistant Editors: Christopher Moore, Jenny Finch
Production Manager: Sophie Chéry
Reprographics: Periplus Publishing London Ltd
Printing: Graphicom, Vicenza

ISBN 1-902699-48-3

PHOTOGRAPHY

BY LENA HERZOG
100 VINTAGE SILVER GELATIN
SELENIUM-TONED PRINTS

THE PHOTOGRAPHS IN THIS BOOK
WERE TAKEN AT THE DANCE
CLASSES AND REHEARSALS OF
YAELISA (CAMINOS FLAMENCOS,
SAN FRANCISCO, USA)
AND MANUELA RÍOS (DANCE
ACADEMY, SEVILLE, SPAIN)

ESSAY

BY IGNACIO DE COSSÍO

FLAMENCO
DANCE CLASS

LENA HERZOG

HISTORY

IGNACIO DE COSSÍO

ORIGINS

Flamenco as an art form is rooted in the fertile mix of Andalucían cultures – Arabic, Jewish, Christian and, of course, Gypsy. This last group, originating in the north of India, is so closely linked to flamenco, that when we study the origin and characteristics of flamenco, we must also look at Romany culture. It is generally believed that the Gypsies, a nomad race par excellence, arrived in Europe in the 15th century. A document signed by King Alfonso V in 1447 authorised the entry of a group of Gypsies into Barcelona. They were perhaps drawn to Andalucía by the warm climate as well as by the hospitality and openness of its inhabitants, accustomed as they were to immigration and invasion by Tartessians, Phoenicians, Greeks, Carthaginians, Romans, Visigoths and Arabs.

Although the Gypsies' contribution to flamenco has been seminal, theirs is by no means the sole influence, as evidenced by the fact that not a single style of singing has been named in the Gypsies' language, Calé. Many flamenco verses derive from ancient Andalucían tradition and folklore, which itself borrowed from a variety of sources.

Flamenco is based on compositions of an instantly recognisable melodic and rhythmic flow, with music that reminds us of Arab cadences, testimony to their presence in Andalucía over many centuries. Its tradition of insistent repetition of periods and languid, melancholic inflections was passed from generation to generation, and lends it a certain Oriental feel reminiscent of the Mozarabic liturgy.

Any attempt to fix accurate historical periods for the development of flamenco must be approximate, since it belongs in the realms of popular culture and oral history. Although there are a few useful literary references, it was not really until 1901, with the invention of the gramophone, that the flamenco legend became history.

As far as we know, the most important singer during the late 18th and early 19th century was Tío Luis 'El de la Juliana', about whom little is recorded, despite the fact that he was considered the leading performer of his time. His contemporary Tío Perico Cantoral was the first recognised professional singer.

The first literary references to the existence of flamenco date from 1793 (Cartas Marruecas, by José Cadalso). And in 1847, with no explanation or elaboration, Serafín Estébanez Calderón 'El Solitario' listed the names of singers such as 'El Planeta' and his disciple Francisco Ortega Vargas 'El Fillo' in Escenas Andaluzas.

The Golden Era

The late 19th to early 20th century was the era of the great figures who established the fundamental styles of flamenco. The man dominating the beginning of this period was the singer Silverio Franconetti, whose surname betrays his Italian origin. Franconetti possessed an extensive repertoire and succeeded in taking flamenco out of its purely Gypsy environment – the smithy and the forge –

performing his art in cafés. Franconetti himself owned the Café de Silverio in the street Rosario de Seville, where he gave performances accompanied by other professional artists. This marked the beginning of flamenco's commercialisation.

During this time, a new branch of flamenco emerged. Starting in Andalucía, it would evolve its greatest expression in the mining areas of the mountains of Cartagena and La Unión (Murcia), due to immigration, principally from Almería. Interest in flamenco was so widespread and the songs and dances so popular, that a street in La Unión could have as many as 10 cafés where singers performed, the most famous owned by Antonio Grau 'El Rojo el Alpargatero'.

Tomás Medrano Vargas 'El Nitri' (the first winner of the Llave de Oro del Cante *award), Enrique 'El Mellizo' and Joaquín 'El de la Paula' also belong to this glorious era, laying the foundations of what today is recognised as the flamenco canon.*

Transition to Flamenco Opera

In this era, it is essential to highlight artists such as Manuel Torre, of whom the poet Federico García Lorca said: "He has more culture in his blood than anyone I have known", Antonio Chacón, who brought flamenco to the theatre stage, and Pastora Pavón 'La Niña de los Peines' and her brother Tomás, who would die bankrupt despite his unsurpassable artistic talents.

This is the period which many see as heralding the decline of flamenco art. A famous musician of the time, Manuel de Falla, backed by a group of intellectuals and artists, organised a contest, the Concurso Nacional de Cante Jondo de Granada, in 1922. For Falla the cante jondo (deep singing) was the purest form, but his contest, instead of promoting this 'purity' in the face of opera's encroachments, only managed to accelerate its decline.

Flamenco Opera (1920-1955)

A lack of purity in the singing translated into superficiality, resulting in an overwrought, elaborate style: the so-called fandango. To this period belong, among others, the payo (non-Gypsy) Pepe Marchena 'Bernardo el de los Lobitos', Rafael Ramos Antúnez 'El Gloria' and Manuel Vallejo.

From 1955 to the present

From 1955 onwards, there was a rediscovery of 'authentic' flamenco thanks to the recording of the first flamenco anthology by Hispavox, the boom of the first tablaos (flamenco bars) and the publication of the book Flamencología by Anselmo González Climent. The Concurso Nacional Arte Flamenco de Córdoba, an influential competition, came to be held every three years and a department of Flamencology was created at the University of Jerez de la Frontera.

The main figures included: Juan Talega 'Tío Gregorio El Borrico', Antonio Cruz García, 'Antonio Mairena', the singer with the longest career in history, José Fernández Granados 'El Perrate de Utrera', Anica 'la Piriñaca', Manolo Caracol, 'La Perla de Cádiz', 'El Sordera de Jerez', 'Agujetas', Bernarda and Fernanda de Utrera, La Paquera de Jerez and, of course, the much lamented José Monge Cruz, popularly known as 'Camarón de la Isla' in reference to his birthplace, the island of San Fernando off Cádiz.

Present-day flamenco is defined by its mixture with other genres, such as pop and blues, typified by groups like Ketama (formed by members of the Carmona dynasty) or artists such as Raimundo Amador, who has played alongside musicians of international stature such as B. B. King. On the other hand, traditional flamenco is also represented by figures like the Gypsy from Jerez, José Mercé, who combines classical forms (soleares, tientos...) with innovative bulerías por fiestas.

When attempting to classify flamenco, it is usual to take the singers as a starting point, since the cante provides the foundation for the guitar and dance. However, dancing and guitar playing have evolved into solo performances in their own right independent of the other components of traditional flamenco. Exceptional guitar players like 'Niño Ricardo', Ramón Montoya, 'Melchor de Marchena', Diego del Gastor, Manuel Morao, Pedro Peña, 'Habichuela', Manolo Sanlúcar, Vicente Amigo, 'Tomatito' and Paco de Lucía (arguably the best and most revolutionary guitar player of all time) have turned flamenco guitar music into a distinct genre.

Meanwhile dancers such as 'La Macarrona', 'Tía Juana la del Pipa', the immortal Carmen Amaya, 'Farruco', Antonio el Pipa, Antonio Ruíz Soler, Eva 'La Yerbabuena' and Sara Baras, among others, are reinventing flamenco dance.

Becoming a flamenco performer is not merely a matter of assimilating knowledge; artists learn their craft, but are also born with it. This dichotomy leads to a division between Gypsies and non-Gypsies when it comes to judging the artistry of flamenco performers. The Gypsies lay claim to a particular talent, a special quality of the voice, a rhythm and peculiar grace of movement, which they say greatly enhances their ability for maximum expression. 'Camarón de la Isla' argued that the Gypsy possesses something denied the payo*: an innate ability that is their birthright. Many great non-gypsy performers have given the lie to these assertions. The* payo *singer Silverio Franconetti and the dancer Sara Baras are cases in point. Maybe as 'Juan Habichuela', the Gypsy guitar player, once said, "you don't have to be either Gypsy or* payo*, just good or bad."*

Above all flamenco is about emotion: laughter or tears. It is the story of the day-to-day life of the soul, with its moments of mad happiness and heartbreaking, bitter lament. It is possible to discern two completely different aspects within flamenco art: the public and joyful mood of the fair, and the sorrowful, intimate encounter in which the innermost human emotions are expressed. At its best, flamenco is a form of communicating tradition while telling a very personal story.

Flamenco lyrics form a separate poetic tradition in Spain, although an artist may change the verses from performance to performance. For example, it is not unknown for a singer to forget the words in the middle of a show and to replace them with stammers and groans without the song losing any of its beauty.

Note the overwhelming sorrow and bitterness in the lyrics of this soleá *(Andalucian folksong and dance):*

Your street is no longer your street,
it could be any street,
on the road to anywhere.
The love you showed me
was dust and sand
carried away by the wind.

Time said to Love:
I will punish you
for that arrogance of yours.

This mountain girl deserved
to be melted down,
like church bells.
Nothing is worse
than the sound,
made by such metal.

I go like a prisoner:

behind me, my shadow;

ahead of me, my thoughts.

The poetic tone of these verses is evident in their style, metre
and rhyme. In fact, it is frequent to find palos, soleares *or* siguiriyas *in*
poems by Andalucían poets, such as Federico García Lorca. On the
other hand, the despair that we find in this soleá *may represent the*
deepest and purest flamenco feeling; that which is accompanied by
the tragic ¡ay!, *which expresses all the fury and anger the human*
heart can bear. Tía Anica 'la Piriñaca' said, "When I sing with emotion,
my mouth tastes of blood."

20

GEOGRAPHY

Flamenco, like Spanish bullfighting, was born in the 'low region' of
Andalucía, that is, the most southerly zone which extends from Seville
to Cádiz. For many aficionados of flamenco, its source is to be found
by following the flow of the Guadalquivir river from the capital of
Andalucía to its mouth on the Atlantic coast of Cádiz. With the river as
its stem, flamenco sends out branches from either bank. The notes of
the song and the power of the dance establish themselves mainly in
the Seville district of Triana, in the regions of Utrera, Lebrija, Écija,
Marchena, Osuna, Carmona, Alcalá de Guadaira and Morón de la
Frontera; in the Cádiz regions of Arcos de la Frontera, Jerez de la
Frontera, Sanlúcar de Barrameda, El Puerto de Santa María, Puerto
Real and San Fernando; and in the city of Cádiz itself. Another

identifiable zone would cover the area between the cities of Seville,
Lucena (Córdoba) and Cádiz.

According to tradition, the cante jondo *was introduced directly to*
the city of Córdoba by the Arab soldiers of Tarik in the 8th century. It is
also interesting to note that a couple of centuries later, an Arab musician
and poet called Ziryab arrived in the Iberian peninsula, bringing
compilations of Persian song that he had listened to along the way. This
imported music was very similar to the seguirillas, soleares, saetas,
malagueñas *and* granadinas, *revealing the Arab and Oriental influences*
on flamenco.

A population census of Andalucía in the 18th century, shows that
the biggest Gypsy settlements corresponded to the two provinces we
have identified as the cradles of flamenco art: Seville and Cádiz. The
presence of the Gypsies decisively influenced the birth and the
development of flamenco. Their preference for marrying their own
kind is shown by the fact that the most common Gypsy surnames
survive to the present day, including flamenco surnames such as
Ortega, Monje, Soto, Vargas, Heredia, Jiménez, Hernández, Reyes,
Montoya, Cruz, Cortés, García, Peña and Santos.

As time passed, flamenco reached a far more extensive area. This
process expanded outwards from an area whose neural centre lies in
Seville-Cádiz. A first line of expansion would include Huelva, north of
Seville, north-east of Córdoba and Málaga. A second line, towards the

east, would include Jaén, Granada and Almería, and finally, a third line
crosses the boundaries of Andalucía to reach Extremadura, south of
Castilla La Mancha and Murcia.

As the area of maximum influence widened, flamenco lost purity
at the expense of a more heterodox approach. According to Luis
López Ruiz, "The original flamenco singing and dancing, at first a
strictly Gypsy phenomenon, later became the traditional singing of
Andalucía per se."

We can complete the map with four basic new areas in which
flamenco song, dance and guitar have taken a strong hold: Salamanca
and Valladolid, where the variations of the Extremaduran flamenco
have taken root; cosmopolitan Madrid with its tablaos; and finally
Barcelona, which received immigrants from Andalucía and
Extremadura owing to its industries. It is in this last city that the
Gypsies developed a new type of rumba *called* rumba catalana, *of*
which Peret is the greatest exponent.

One of the greatest routes of flamenco that must be followed
today by any aficionado starts at Utrera and Lebrija, 30 and 70km from
Seville, respectively. The poet José María de Pemán said of the village
of Lebrija that it was founded by men who died on the cross singing
soleares. *Jerez de la Frontera, 30km from Cádiz, lays claim to the best*
singing, together with the Andalucían provinces of Almería, Córdoba,
Granada and Jaén.

BEGINNERS' CLASS

8:00-11:00

I go like a prisoner:
Behind me, my shadow;
ahead of me, my thoughts

Lyrics from a *soleá*

Dancers are in a continual trance

Eva 'La Yerbabuena'

*These legs of mine that once
were made of bronze are
turning into wire*

Juana Vargas 'La Macarrona'

CHAPTER TWO

INTERMEDIATE

12:00 -15:00

*You want me to tell
you about dancing?
I don't even know myself!*

Carmen Amaya

*You need a Black sound
to work the magic*

Manuel Torre

When I die remember what I asked –
that with your locks of black hair
you tie up my hands

Lyrics from a *siguiria*

*I am more Gypsy than
the ribs of the Pharaoh*

Tía Juana la del Pipa

*We go from venue to venue,
hoping to find a kind soul
who remembers flamenco ...
they don't even want us in
the cafes, we who were always
treated like queens*

Juana Vergas 'La Macarrona'

CHAPTER THREE

ADVANCED
REHEARSAL
15:00-18:00

Dancing, in the strict sense of the word, has to be performed from the waist up

Pastora Imperio

I become a sculpture of fire

Pastora Imperio

Cayetana Alba could have been another Carmen Amaya, had she not lost her way and become an aristocrat

Enrique 'El Cojo'

PERFORMANCE

IGNACIO DE COSSÍO

The poet Fernando Quiñones said, "One does not understand the cante [song] one lives it." This characteristic of the cante *takes us back to the idea of flamenco as an expression of emotion, and to the importance of being able to understand what the artist is trying to convey.*

CANTE

To learn about the cante, *the potential aficionado must have patience and be able to distinguish between the different styles and rhythms. Experts in flamenco* cante *must listen to many singers before laying claim to authority.*

Flamenco cante *developed and extended over new areas largely by word of mouth. Except in very rare circumstances, the music was never written down, and it is not surprising that there are many guitar players who say they accompany the singer by ear. Some verses have only recently been recorded for posterity. Andalusian poets have also contributed to the flamenco opus by writing verses for the* cante. *One example is this rueful* siguiriya *composed by the poet, Manuel Machado, from Seville.*

Rather than being a poet,
my first desire
would have been
to be a good *banderillero*.

The different cantes *can be classified as follows: the basic* cantes, fandangos *and their derivatives;* cante grande *(big);* cante chico *(little); songs that you can dance to and those that you can't. However, our classification is based on specific* palos *(styles) that can be danced to, grouping these together with their different variations. The majority of these variations are due to geography or to the whims of personal style. Songs that are currently being performed can be divided into the following three groups:*

Basic songs and their derivatives

Siguiriya: *(also* seguiriya *or* seguirilla*) this is considered to be one of the original forms and is accompanied by guitar and dance. The* siguiriya *is a profound and dramatic song, which is quite difficult to interpret. As a result, the accompanying dance tends to assume its mood of solemnity and is slow, halting and dry. A very popular variation is the Gypsy* siguiriya*:*

> When I die,
> remember what I asked…
> that with your locks of black hair
> you tie up my hands.

Soleares: *(also* soleá*) is made up of three or four verses that can be accompanied by a dance that is slow and sumptuous. The* soleá *is another of the basic pillars of flamenco* cante *and, like the* siguiriya, tonás *and* tango, *is considered purely Gypsy. It is written in 3/8 time in a minor key, sometimes modulated to its relative major, with a brief pause in the subdominant of the minor key before beginning anew.*

Bridge of Triana!
The balustrade crashed
with the cart that was carrying her!

Tango: *a cheerful song from Cádiz that accompanies the dance. It is composed of three or four verses, and accompanied by the strum of the guitar. Its dance is joyful, graceful, insinuating and at times also quite improvisational.*

Before the altar you vowed
that you would never forget me;
but you broke that vow
when I most needed you.

Tanguillo: *has no fixed measure but does have a chorus that gives it a lively structure. It is a song native to Cádiz, full of the burlesque tone which characterises that city's carnival. It is accompanied by guitar and dance and, as with the* tango, *it includes improvisations. One of the most popular from Cádiz is about a type of coin, the 'duros':*

Those ancient duros
set tongues wagging in Cádiz.

People were finding them

on the seashore.

It was the funniest thing

that you can imagine:

half of Cádiz was there with their pickaxes

even my mother-in-law,

even though she was nearly senile [...]

Tiento: *attributed to the singer from Cádiz, Enrique 'El Mellizo'. It consists of three or four verses, accompanied by guitar and dance, and is quite melodious despite its slow solemnity:*

When I go to my room

I speak to God and say to him

that it seems incredible

what you have done to me.

Polo: *a song of four octosyllabic verses with rhyming couplets, which is sometimes confused with the* caña. *It is accompanied by guitar and dance and is written in 3/8 time. The tempo is* allegro moderato, *allowing a great variety of rhythms.*

They ask me if I love you.

I am weighed down by hardships;

I love you

as I love myself.

Caña: *similar to the* polo, *it was considered impossible to dance until Carmen Amaya introduced it to her repertoire. The artist who interpreted it best was Antonio Chacón:*

> They can order me
> to serve my God and country,
> but there is no law
> that can make me leave you.

Liviana: *a Gypsy song that is halfway between the* siguiriya *and the* serrana. *Its structure consists of four verses, accompanied by guitar and danced with solemnity. Its best exponent was Antonio Mairena.*

> Those who want berries from the *madroño* tree
> should go to the mountains,
> as all the fruit is falling
> from the boughs.

Serrana: *song of farmers, bandits, mule-drivers and shepherds. Its structure is the same as that of the* liviana *with the addition of a chorus, usually followed by a typical series ending with a* siguiriya. *It is accompanied by guitar and the dance is a recent innovation.*

> Through Sierra Morena
> a group of soldiers advances,
> their captain is José María.

He will not be made prisoner
so long as his dapple-grey pony
holds up its head.

Romance: (also corrido or corrida) *is the product of Gypsies and Andalusians living side by side, which resulted in the traditional Castilian romance being influenced by flamenco music. Originally it was not danced to, but in the version of singer Antonio Mairena, it can be danced as a* bulería.

My mother sent me to a convent
so she could keep my dowry.
I was seized by four people
and put in a cart,
they took me through the villages
and over and over
I said good-bye
to my friends [...]

Cantiña: *a generic name which includes* alegrías, romeras, mirabrás *and* caracoles. Alegrías *stand out by dint of their gracefulness, and those from Cádiz are the most popular. They were mainly composed as accompaniment to the dances performed at fairs.*

Ay! My heart,
anyone who says that he doesn't feel

pain in his heart

doesn't have a heart

with which to feel.

The heart is in pain,

when it lives

without trust.

The romera gets its name from the repeated reference within the stanza to a pilgrim girl and her loved one. As with all the other cantiñas, it is a song with guitar accompaniment, that is very cheerful and easy to dance.

Pilgrim girl! Ay, my pilgrim girl!

Don't sing me any more songs.

If I catch you in the fray,

not even your mother can save you.

The mirabrás is a vibrant song for guitar performed at fairs. Its composition and subject matter echo the proclamations of town criers. Historically, it is linked to the liberal movement which began in Cádiz with the creation of a parliament in 1812.

I don't care

if a king should condemn me,

when all the people are behind me.

The voice of the people is the voice of God.

Deeds are the living truth,
singing the *mirabrás*
she ties her hair
with a black thread.

Caracoles *owe their name to the chorus that repeats this word in
the manner of a proclamation. The dance is usually performed by
women, as it demands certain undulating movements which would be
very difficult for a man.*

From Sanlúcar to Puerto
there is a highway,
travelled by the Mirris
there and back.
The small Mirri,
the large Mirri,
both made
of candy sugar.
What is that sound?
The prisoners
in their chains.

Petenera: *each stanza has four verses, some repeated, so that six
verses are usually sung. The accompaniment is in 6/8 time and
composed with distinct variations. It is sung and danced in a gradually
building tempo, with majesty, arrogance and sensuality.*

Whoever called you Petenera
got it wrong.
They should have called you
the 'ruin of men'.

Bulería: *the festive song of the Jerez Gypsies. Two basic types should*
be highlighted: the bulerías al golpe, *to be sung; and the* bulerías
ligadas, *to be danced.*

Yesterday in the street your daughter
asked me to kiss her.
It sent a chill through me –
she has your face.
And I shook all over
from the sadness I felt
to think she was so beautiful
she could be our daughter.

Fandango *and its derivatives*

Fandango: *its origins are unclear, although it appears, strangely*
enough, that it was first intended to accompany the dance, which
consists of three tempos with lively and passionate movements.

You keep me under control
even the water that I drink;

I don't know how all this will end
with your damned jealousy.

Fandanguillo: *type of song originating in Huelva, which in the old days used to accompany the* fandango. *It is, however, more spectacular and colourful and is sung at full voice.*

Between the mountain and the marshland
there is a hidden star.
And if my eyes don't deceive me
it is the Virgen del Rocío,
the most beautiful in Spain.

Verdiale: *this name is derived from the village where the song originates. The stanza has four octosyllabic verses and is sung and danced to a guitar, frequently accompanied by violin, castanets and even whistles to mark the beat. Its style is simple and cheerful; the most popular are the* verdiales *by the* cantaor *Juan Breva.*

Ay, village of Los Verdiales!
Who could carry you
tucked in a pouch
like a folded piece of paper?

Jabera: *this is a highly elaborate four-verse stanza without metre, the dance for which demands a high level of stamina:*

Why don't you forget me today,

since you're going to forget me tomorrow?

Put me out of my misery,

don't be so wicked, gypsy girl.

Rondeña: *the oldest* fandango *in Málaga, with four verses. The* rondeña *dance is lively, with a profusion of twirls:*

You came singing a *Rondeña*,

I sit on my bed,

because, when I hear *rondeñas*,

it lightens my heart.

Taranto: *five-verse song with a mining theme and insistent rhythm which is accompanied by guitar and dance.*

The mayor of Guadix

proclaimed an edict:

the stalks of corn

should not be dragged along the ground

because they still need to be used.

Regional and Latin-American folkloric songs

Sevillana: *song to accompany a dance originating in Seville and which is very popular in Andalucia. The dance is performed by couples, mixed or two women, in a series of four songs known as* primera, segunda, tercera *and* cuarta, *all of them with different lyrics and steps, but with a common chorus. They can be lively and cheerful, or slow with lingering movements:*

> María is my reason for living
> I would die for her.
> Dolores cries for me,
> but I don't love her.
> They are night and day
> my two loves,
> the love of María
> and that of Dolores.

Villancico: *a four-verse song which the singer introduces while narrating a Christmas story. Nowadays they are often sung in the style of* bulerías *or* fiestas *that can be danced to.*

> The Virgin has a rose
> on her divine breast,
> given to her by San José
> before the Child was born.

Joy, joy, joy,

joy, joy, joy,

the Virgin Mary has given birth

in a Bethlehem stable!

Farruca: *a kind of* tango *from Cádiz with four verses full of cadence and melancholy. The fact that it is a severe, haughty and sober dance makes it particularly suitable for men, its defining characteristic being the drumming and tapping of the heels.*

An immigrant girl in Galicia

was crying bitterly,

because the immigrant boy

who played the bagpipes for her was dead.

Garrotín: *the dancer-singer marks the beat by clicking their fingers. This is a festive Gypsy song and dance, with simple lyrics and repeated chorus. It became very popular thanks to 'La Niña de los Peines'.*

Ask my hat,

my hat will tell you

about the bad night it is having

and the cold night air.

Garrotín, singing the *garrotín*,

on the river, river, river bank

of San Juan ...

Rumba: *a four-verse song of Spanish/Cuban origin. It is a song that travelled – a Spanish song exported to America, where it was influenced by local folklore before returning to Spain heavily modified. A very popular version is that of the Catalan Gypsies, notably performed by Peret.*

> I took her home
> and introduced her to my family,
> and they put a crown on her head
> for being a good gypsy girl.

Zambra: *a very old song with a repetitive and monotonous rhythm. The* zambra *has four verses, and nowadays it is possible to see it danced in the Sacromonte caves in Granada.*

> You called me 'bitter herb'
> this name is hurtful to me,
> your love has no equal,
> you will drive me to my grave.

THE DANCE

As we saw in the previous section, in which we analysed the cante, *the dance developed as its accompaniment, to further express the torrent of emotions conjured by the* cante. *As with the* cante, *there is no denying the special talent of Gypsy performers, but* payos, *mostly from Andalucia, both in the past and present, have brought* spectacular skill to the dance. The principal characteristic of Gypsy dance is its lack of academicism, its reliance on intuition and personal style; whilst payo dance tends to proceed from instruction, concentrating on polished technique whilst retaining the essential flamenco spirit.

The first literary references to flamenco dance are found in Escenas Andaluzas by Estébanez Calderón, in particular to a dance from the Triana quarter of Seville, from where the Cava de los Gitanos promulgated flamenco to the city. The emergence of flamenco in general, and of dance in particular, probably goes back much further, but with no written records, it is dangerous to speculate. Flamenco dance is probably easier for the novice to appreciate than the cante. In the present era, with its emphasis on the visual, flamenco dance is fast gaining in popularity, with its zapateados (toe and heel clicking), its lithe wrist and waist movements, and upright, defiant torsos full of feeling and fury. The dancers are blessed with a divine talent capable of captivating any audience, which is why they are appreciated by foreigners. As a result the dance has become the form of flamenco expression most frequently seen on stages all over the world, to such an extent that it is no longer a sub-genre of the cante, but an art form in its own right.

The main stylistic differentiation in flamenco dance is between the male and female, although nowadays there is a tendency towards a more homogeneous dance as a result of the intermingling of the *styles of both sexes. However, the essence of both male and female dance is an inborn grace, independent of gender. Tomás Pavón said with reference to the* cante*: "The* cante jondo *is neither taught nor learnt, it is perfected", this applies to all forms of flamenco. Personality, magic, grace, innate art and* ángel *(spirit) must all be part of the basic stock of any male or female dancer, because technical precision means nothing if you don't feel the dance from within.*

The male dance is characterised by its command of the upright posture, by the foot stamping and by the strength of the arms. Hand movements are usually considered less important for the male dancers, although in the case of Gypsy dance they acquire a greater prominence.

As might be expected, costumes have changed over time, tending towards simplification and modernisation. The traditional long-tailed dresses, which could often hamper the dancer, are no longer worn. Nowadays, tight-fitting dresses have become the fashion, allowing appreciation of the arm movements, along with long, wide satin skirts, which the dancer controls gracefully as she stamps her heels. The colourful male costumes have also been discarded in favour of tight trousers and dark jackets; even a bare chest in the case of the dancer Joaquín Cortés.

In the end, flamenco dance is set apart by the deliberation of its movements. As the dancer Manuela Vargas said, "you must dwell a little in the performance." Flamenco dance is not a competition based on the number of steps you can perform in a minute. It does not require a large space to perform; the art consists in knowing how to move within the space of a couple of floor tiles.

Given the close link between the cante *and the dance, it is important to know what kind of song is being performed and directing the dance. It is for this reason that we dedicated so many words to the* cante *and its different variations and styles; without it, the dance would not exist. Nowadays there is an unfortunate tendency to mix styles indiscriminately.*

Since time immemorial, serious and lighter songs have been combined – earlier we mentioned this with regard to siguiriyas, livianas *and* serranas *– however, it is one thing to try and lighten the drama and another to mix styles on a whim, which can seriously detract from the integrity of the dance. Maybe it is up to the public to insist on authenticity, but this would presuppose an educated audience.*

DUENDE *AND* ÁNGEL

In the Dictionary of the Real Academia Española, *the term* duende *applied to flamenco is defined as 'mysterious and elusive magic'. The Gypsy singer Sordera de Jerez was right:* "Duende *is something within, nobody can know it, it must come from the individual."*
It is, by its nature, intangible. The singer Manolo Caracol said, "Who knows what duende *is? If one only knew, one could say:* Duende, come now."

You may take duende *to mean some kind of supernatural inspiration that leads the guitar player, the dancer and the singer to interpret their art with such a power of expression that they may rip their clothes or scratch themselves in its thrall. It is, taken all in all, the sublimation of flamenco art, and the greatest suffering for any artist is to find that they have been deserted by the* duende.

When an artist is touched by the duende, *they attain a quality and emotion in their* cante, *dance and playing that seem to come from another sphere. It is then they feel at ease and really communicate emotion, but it is the performer's essence, their innate grace or magic touch that holds the audience and sends a shiver up the spine, in other words, the* ángel. *An artist who has this essence and who is possessed by the* duende *surpasses the limits of the human and transforms flamenco into something divine. In other words, the* duende *is the soul, and the* ángel *is the body.*

THE NEW FLAMENCO

The dancer Antonio Canales claimed,"it is now considered bad taste to say you dislike flamenco, whereas 10 years ago it was bad taste to admit you did." Flamenco has come back from deepest oblivion to reinstate itself as a highly fashionable genre. There are now styles we could call 'new flamenco' based on a fusion with other genres, such as pop and blues.

The path that has brought about this symbiosis of genres has been long and arduous. The first steps towards new flamenco can be traced to the singer Camarón de la Isla, the guitar player 'Paco de Lucía' and the dancer Antonio Gades.

The Camarón-'Paco de Lucía' duo was one of the most innovative of the 70s. 'Paco de Lucía' succeeded in expanding the horizons of Andalusian guitar with his fusion-flamenco, which allowed him to come into contact with the jazz players Chick Korea, Jorge Pardo, Carles Benavent and Rubém Dantas, and the classical music of the Spanish composer Manuel de Falla, and, last but not least, musicians of international standing such as Carlos Santana. Camarón de la Isla became known as the 'Mick Jagger of Cádiz' for his flouting of orthodox flamenco strictures.

At this same time, the dancer Antonio Gades combined flamenco with classical ballet, giving his dance a wholly contemporary feel, typified by his adaptation of the play Bodas de Sangre by Federico García Lorca.

These artists paved the way for a climate of receptivity within flamenco, which would culminate in new styles and the creation of what could be called 'flamenco-pop'. The pioneers of this genre were Las Greças who with Te estoy amando locamente (I love you madly), their dyed blond hair and their bright disco outfits, broke with the Gypsy myth and with convention. These women were followed by other very successful groups such as Los Chorbos, Los Chichos o Los

Chunguitos, who won over all kinds of audiences with their rumba-pop, and Pata Negra, of whom Camarón said, "Pata Negra has achieved what we are all looking for: Gypsy flamenco-rock". Another kind of rumba, more Catalan in flavour, would be interpreted by Peret and by the international Gypsy Kings, a genre that also spread far within the pop scene.

Currently, Raimundo Amador and the groups Ketama and the Barbería del Sur, are in the vanguard of experimental fusion with jazz and blues, begun in his time by the guitar player Paco de Lucía.

Some purists have been unable or unwilling to understand this new wave, which doesn't necessarily constitute a threat to traditional flamenco. Ketama realise that aficionados do not consider their music to be flamenco, because it is not rooted in tradition, but that doesn't mean it isn't music of quality. According to the writer Antonio Gala: "Flamenco, despite the risks, will always remain pure, because the mystery will protect itself."

There is not the least doubt that flamenco in all its aspects is expanding from its origins in local tradition into an export product. Its lyrics are gradually changing from purely poetic expression, to storytelling and in some cases to the narration of an event; poetry giving way to prose with a journalistic slant. So much so, that the lyrics give the place, time and date as the story develops through the faltering voice of the cantaor. The woman is almost always guilty in all the tragedies and the man is alone, cast in a pathetic light, while the woman pursues her dance indifferent to the passionate conflict. It is all so actual, so real, that we seem invited to sing and dance under the spell of an unceasing rhythm, seemingly forever reinventing itself. It is an eruption of feeling which not even a radical jazz-band can reproduce. Unfaithful women, abandoned men, orgies of sorrow, alcohol-fuelled emotions, miners down the pit, prisoners and prison guards parade fleetingly before us. Life itself, going incessantly round and round, while in the air, hands, feet and voice remain unyielding, transporting us to the deepest part of the cante; *the background noise of a hammer in the smithy hitting a red-hot knife that threatens to jump out at us.*

BEGINNERS' CLASS
8:00-11:00

Before the class

"Class!"

Learning turns 1, 2, 3

Learning turns 4, 5

Learning turns 6

"Stop!"

Dancer and a piano

Upper body stretch

Teaching *sevillanas*

Turning

An uncertain move

Tango exercise

Skirt, leg and a castanet

Yaelisa

A sudden stop

Learning rhythm

Main position

Bulería

Teaching precision
(Manuela Ríos)

A difficult move

"Like this!"

Build up to a break
1, 2, 3

Break – a big movement

From the waist up 1, 2

Going across the floor

Turns with castanets

Dancer with castanets

Watching the teacher

INTERMEDIATE
12:00-15:00

Mid-class break

Instruction

Class at noon

Facing the windows

Two dancers

Yaelisa and three
students

From the waist up 3, 4

Going forward

Tanguillo

Flores

Dancer

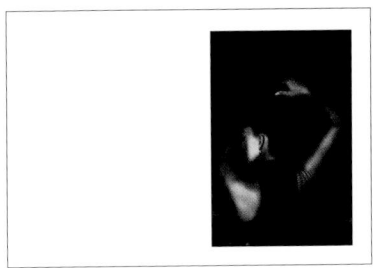

Arms exercise 1, 2, 3, 4

Silencio

Legs

Tilting

Teaching *soleá*

Dance class

Learning posture

Dancer and teacher

¡Arriba!

Exercise with castanets

Learning skirt moves

"Preparation!"

Dancers and the mirror

Bulería moves 1

Bulería moves 2

Dancer without a face

Teacher

A *sevillana* move

Sevillana 2

End of the third hour

ADVANCED CLASS
15:00-18:00

Alignment

Four dancers

Last shape

A quiet start

Alegria

Footwork

Fast turns 1, 2

A *soleá* move

Swirl of skirt

Following the teacher

Spotting

Fast move

Leg stretch

Balance in motion

Dancers and sharp shadows

Assignment

Long stretch

Dancer at the window

Defne 1, 2, 3, 4

End

LENA HERZOG

Born and raised in Siberia, Herzog studied
Linguistics at the University of Saint Petersburg,
Russia, and graduated with a degree in Philosophy
from Mills College, California.

Arcperiplus has published two earlier volumes
of her photographs,
TAUROMAQUIA and *PILGRIMS.*

IGNACIO DE COSSÍO

Born in Seville, de Cossío changed from studying
Veterinary Medicine in Caceres to Journalism
at the University of Wales in Seville, and now works
in radio and the media. Previous works
are *COSSÍO Y LOS TOROS* and *LES GRANDES
FAENAS DEL SIGLO XX*, both published
by Espasa-Calpe.